FREEDOM'S
PROMISE

MARCH FONG EU
ACTIVIST AND POLITICIAN

BY DUCHESS HARRIS, JD, PHD

WITH SAMANTHA S. BELL

Core Library

An Imprint of Abdo Publishing
abdobooks.com

Cover image: March Fong Eu was passionate about
women's rights issues.

Cover Photo: George Rose/Hulton Archive/Getty Images
Interior Photos: George Rose/Hulton Archive/Getty Images, 1; Paul Sakuma/AP Images, 5;
AP Images, 6–7, 37; Walter Zeboski/AP Images, 9, 43; David Fenton/Archive Photos/Getty
Images, 10; David Bransby/Farm Security Administration - Office of War Information Photograph
Collection/Library of Congress, 12; Frederic Lewis/Archive Photos/Getty Images, 16–17; Red Line
Editorial, 20, 27; John S Lander/LightRocket/Getty Images, 24–25; Al Amy/New York Daily News
Archive/Getty Images, 30; Rich Pedroncelli/AP Images, 32–33; Cook/AP Images, 35; Nick Ut/AP
Images, 38

Editor: Maddie Spalding
Series Designer: Ryan Gale

Library of Congress Control Number: 2019942001

Publisher's Cataloging-in-Publication Data

Names: Harris, Duchess, author. | Bell, Samantha S., author.
Title: March Fong Eu: activist and politician / by Duchess Harris and Samantha S. Bell
Other title: activist and politician
Description: Minneapolis, Minnesota : Abdo Publishing, 2020 | Series: Freedom's promise |
Includes online resources and index.
Identifiers: ISBN 9781532190865 (lib. bdg.) | ISBN 9781532176715 (ebook)
Subjects: LCSH: Eu, March Fong--Juvenile literature. | Women legislators--United States--
Biography--Juvenile literature. | Asian American legislators--Biography--Juvenile
literature. | California Secretary of State--Biography--Juvenile literature. |
Ambassadors--United States--Biography--Juvenile literature.
Classification: DDC 328.73 [B]--dc23

CONTENTS

A LETTER FROM DUCHESS

Political leaders often take action to draw attention to their causes. In 1969 politician March Fong Eu did something no one had ever done before. She smashed a toilet outside the California State Capitol building. She wanted to raise awareness of gender discrimination. At the time, women had to pay to use toilets in public places. Certain toilets for men were free to use. Her action captured the attention of people around the world.

Eu accomplished remarkable things in her political career. She was passionate about women's rights, education, and many other issues. She was the first Asian American woman elected to the California State Assembly. She was later the first woman to serve as California's secretary of state. She faced discrimination, but she was determined to overcome all obstacles in her path.

Please join me on a journey to learn about this pioneering and influential woman. Eu left a legacy that has inspired others who have benefited from her promise of freedom.

Duchess Harris

March Fong Eu's political career spanned more than 20 years.

CHAPTER ONE

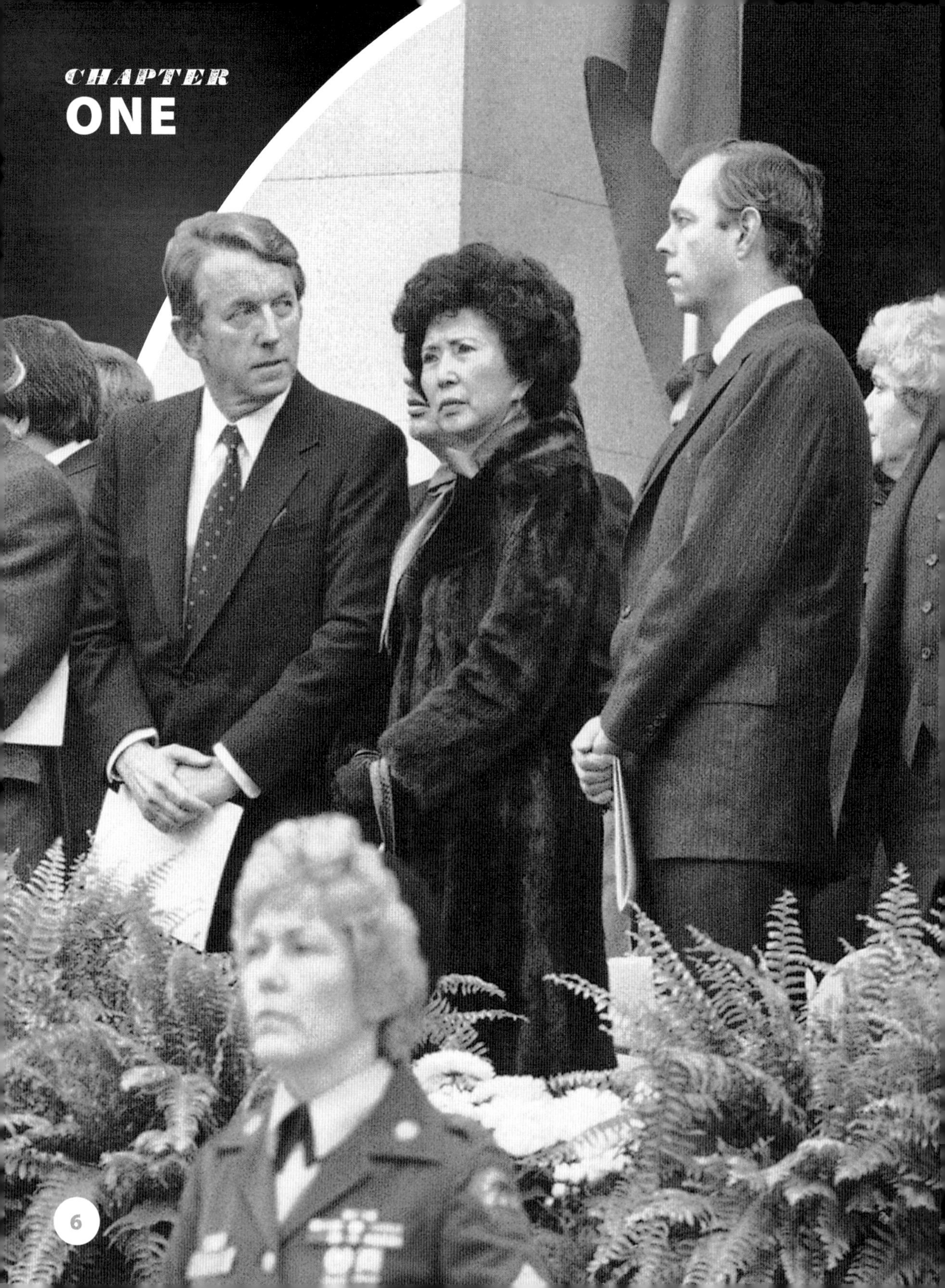

MAKING A POINT

I n April 1969, March Fong Eu introduced a bill to the California State Assembly. Eu was a member of this governing body. Her bill involved pay toilets. At the time, people had to pay to use toilets in public buildings. But urinals, a type of toilet for men, were usually free. Eu believed this was a form of gender discrimination. Eu's bill would make all public toilets free to use.

The California State Assembly is one part of the California State Legislature. The other part is the California State Senate. The legislature makes the laws for the state. Eu was the first Asian American woman to

Eu, *second from left*, stands with other California leaders in 1983.

serve in the California State Assembly. She was elected to the assembly in 1966.

First Eu's bill had to go to a committee. The committee members would discuss the bill. They could pass it or defeat it. If Eu's bill passed, it would go back to the assembly and the senate for a vote. Other legislators had tried to pass bills to make public toilets free before. But their bills did not make it out of the committee. Eu hoped her bill would pass.

Eu's supporters organized a protest parade on the day the bill was to be heard in the committee. They marched up the steps of the California State Capitol building in Sacramento. At the top of the steps was a toilet. It was wrapped in a fake chain and lock. Eu picked up a sledgehammer and smashed the toilet. She wanted to show people she would fight injustice.

Newspapers around the United States reported the event. Other countries reported it as well. Eu's bill did

Eu smashed a toilet as a symbolic gesture against gender inequality.

not make it out of the committee. But she helped more people understand the issue.

To Eu, pay toilets were a small problem. She knew there were bigger issues to fix. But she believed it was

The women's rights movement gained momentum in the 1960s.

important to fight all forms of gender discrimination. At the time, many women were trying to gain equal rights. They were part of the women's rights movement. The pay-toilets protest showed the world that American women wanted to be treated fairly.

THE CHANGING ROLES OF WOMEN

The gender discrimination Eu fought had been part of American culture for a long time. Before World War II (1939–1945), most married middle- and upper-income white women were homemakers. They did household chores such as cleaning and cooking. They shopped for groceries and took care of their children. Jobs were limited for women who wanted to work outside the home. Often they were only able to find jobs as secretaries or department store clerks. Women of color and women who lived in poverty had even fewer opportunities.

When the United States entered World War II in 1941, many men went off to war. Women had to fill the jobs they left behind. They became government and office workers. They operated streetcars

WE CAN DO IT!

Approximately 6 million American women joined the workforce during World War II. Some of them made weapons and equipment. Artist Norman Rockwell created a painting of one of these women for the cover of a magazine. The painting featured a woman with a tool called a rivet gun. Rivet guns are used to attach pieces of metal together. The woman became known as Rosie the Riveter. Another popular image showed Rosie wearing a bandana and flexing her muscles. In the picture, Rosie says, "We can do it!" Rosie became a symbol of the wartime sacrifices many women made. She is also a symbol of women's strength and skill.

During World War II, many women built military equipment such as airplanes in factories.

and drove taxis. Women also took on jobs to support the war effort. They built weapons and other military equipment. They worked in factories. They gained new skills and confidence.

After the war ended in 1945, people expected women to leave the workforce. But many women wanted to keep working. Some enjoyed earning their own money. This made them feel independent and self-reliant. Others wanted to keep working because they needed the extra income. Between 1940 and 1960, the number of married, working women more than doubled.

THE NEED FOR EQUALITY

Despite these changes, women still did not have the same rights and opportunities as men. In the 1960s, a bank could refuse to give a credit card to an unmarried woman. If a woman was married, banks could require her credit card to have her husband's signature. Many states did not allow women to serve on juries. Employers paid women less money than men. This gender pay gap persists today.

In 1961 President John F. Kennedy created the President's Commission on the Status of Women (PCSW). It was made up of labor unions, government agencies, and women's organizations. Former First Lady Eleanor Roosevelt led the commission. It studied women's involvement in politics and the economy.

It came up with ideas to get more women involved in these areas. However, it did not study all women. It ignored some women of color, including Asian, Latina, and Native American women.

In 1963 the PCSW published a report. It found that women earned 59 cents for every dollar that a man earned. They were unable to advance in most jobs. They had to settle for lower-paying positions.

Eu recognized these issues. She supported women's equality. She faced discrimination as both a woman and an Asian American. Male legislators made fun of her after the toilet-smashing incident.

Eu's efforts brought widespread attention to the pay-toilet issue. Her activism inspired California governor Ronald Reagan. In 1974 he signed a bill that banned paid public toilets. Six weeks later, Eu became California's secretary of state. The pay-toilet ban was just one part of her impressive legacy.

EXPLORE ONLINE

Chapter One discusses the changing roles of women during World War II. The article at the website below goes into more depth on this topic. Compare the information on this website with the information provided in Chapter One. What new information did you learn from the website?

THE WAR: FAMILY
abdocorelibrary.com/march-fong-eu

CHAPTER TWO

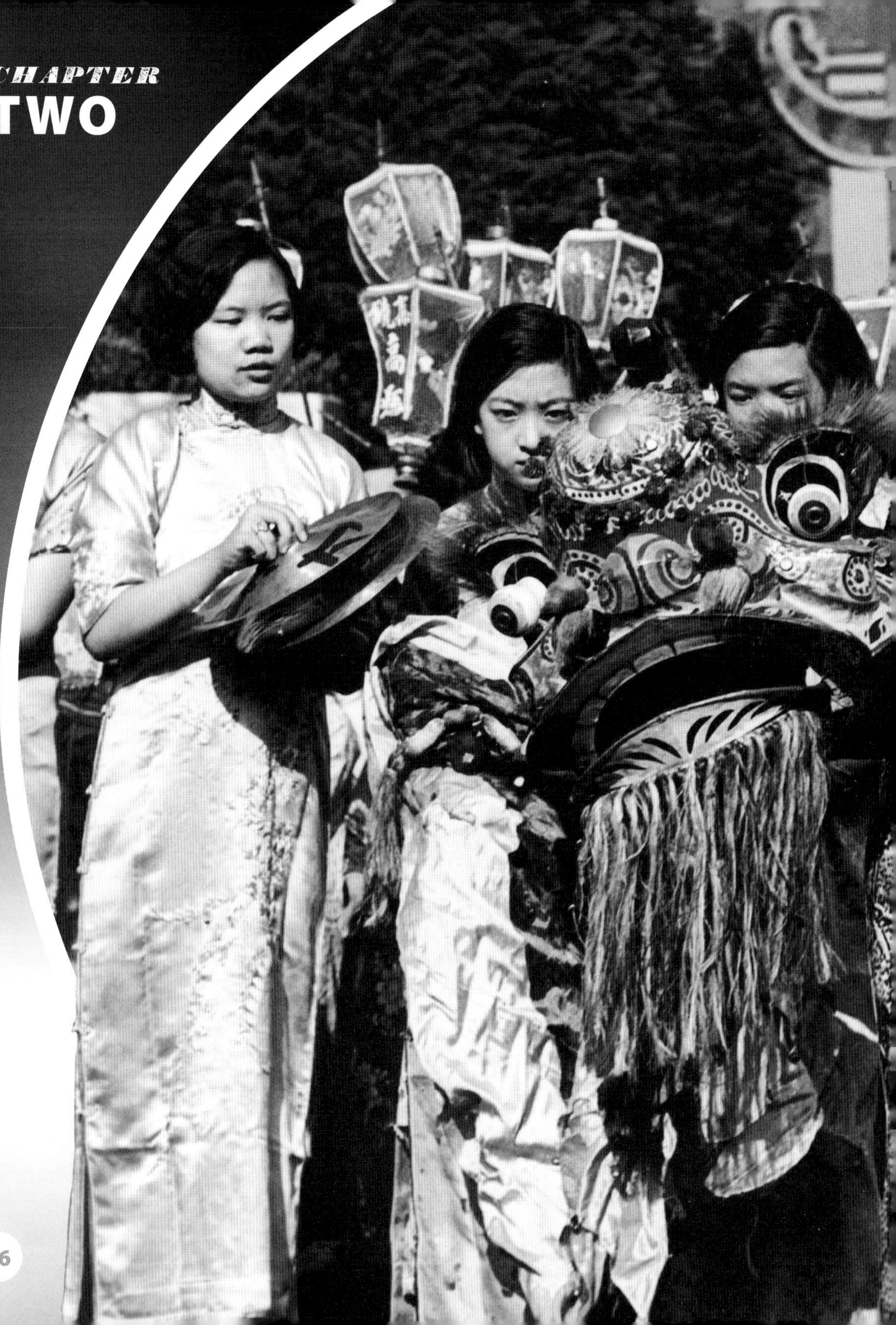

A GOOD EDUCATION

Eu was born March Kong on March 29, 1922, in Oakdale, California. Her mother was a Chinese immigrant who had never been to school. She had not learned how to read or write. She did not speak any English. March's father was also Chinese American. He had been born in the United States. He had attended school for four years. He spoke a little English.

March was the youngest of four children. She had an older sister and two older brothers.

In the early 1900s, many Chinese Americans preserved their Chinese cultures through traditional art and ceremonies.

They spoke Chinese with their parents. But they talked to each other in English.

March's parents had a laundry business. They worked hard every day washing and ironing clothes. March and her family lived in the back of the laundry.

After March was born, her parents decided to move the family to Richmond, California. They continued to work in the laundry business. They again lived in the back of their laundry. Richmond was a small town. March and her family were the only Chinese Americans in the area.

March became involved in many school activities. In junior high school, she was the editor of the school newspaper. In both junior high and high school, she participated in sports. She also joined the honor society and became a cheerleader.

March was concerned about her parents' money struggles. She wanted a better life for her parents. She realized that a good education could help change

her circumstances.
She also wanted to
help other people in
similar situations. She
learned all she could
in school. She studied
hard to become a
straight-A student.

CHOOSING A CAREER

March did well in math
and science classes.
She enjoyed learning
about soil and farming.
She thought about
becoming a chemist.
One day, March talked
with her school bus
driver about her plan.
The bus driver thought

PERSPECTIVES

IMMIGRATION RESTRICTIONS

In the 1850s, March's grandfather and many other Chinese immigrants came to California. Gold had been discovered there. Many immigrants became miners. They later found jobs as farmhands, servants, and railroad workers. But white Americans grew more hostile toward them as fewer jobs became available. In 1882 the US Congress severely restricted immigration from China. Immigration continued to be restricted until 1965. In that year, President Lyndon B. Johnson signed the Immigration and Nationality Act. He said the new law would "repair a very deep and painful flaw in the fabric of American justice."

GENDER BARRIERS IN EDUCATION

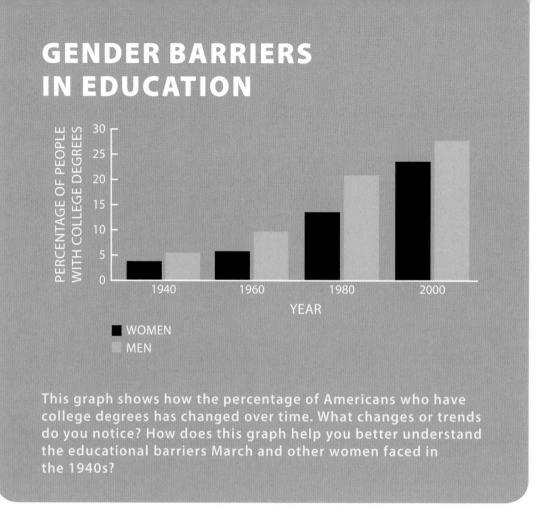

This graph shows how the percentage of Americans who have college degrees has changed over time. What changes or trends do you notice? How does this graph help you better understand the educational barriers March and other women faced in the 1940s?

it was a good idea because she could go back to China to help Chinese people. March realized the bus driver did not think she belonged in the United States.

March had also considered teaching as a career. But when she was in high school, the school counselor told her not to go into education. The counselor said it would be very difficult for March to get a teaching job. She said no one would hire a Chinese teacher.

Despite this discrimination, March was not discouraged. She had always planned to go to college. Her sister and one of her brothers had gone to college. Her other brother became a businessman. He bought a store in Gilroy, California. Her parents sold their laundry business, and the family moved to Gilroy. They helped March's brother with his business. March had just finished high school. She was dating a dental student named Chester Fong. He told her there were opportunities in dentistry. She could become a dental hygienist. Dental hygienists assist dentists. March attended nearby Salinas Junior College for her first year of college. She studied dental hygiene.

After one year at Salinas, March moved on to the University of California, Berkeley. She also studied at the University of California, San Francisco. She worked during the summer to pay for her classes. During the school year, she worked as a nanny. She helped mothers take care of their children. In exchange, they gave her a room and meals.

THE CHINESE YOUNG LADIES' SOCIETY

During World War II, many Chinese Americans joined the armed services. March's husband was among those who joined. March knew other Chinese women who had husbands serving abroad. She organized the Chinese Young Ladies' Society so they could get together and support each other. The group also included young women who were not married. The society hosted parties for Chinese American soldiers who were stationed in the area.

MORE TO LEARN

While March was still in college, Chester finished school and started a dental practice. Then Chester and March married. March graduated from the University of California, Berkeley, in 1943 with a degree in dentistry. By then, Chester had gone into the military. March found a part-time job as a dental hygienist.

March later began working full-time as a dental hygienist within the public school system in Oakland, California. After she had worked one year in that job, the University of California, San Francisco, offered her a position. She was asked to help with the school's teaching program. She continued to work as a dental hygienist in Oakland schools while she helped the university.

FURTHER EVIDENCE

Chapter Two discusses March's childhood and the obstacles Chinese Americans faced in the early 1900s. What is one of the main points of this chapter? What evidence supports this point? Read the article at the website below. Does the information on the website support the point you identified? Or does it present new evidence?

CHINATOWN
abdocorelibrary.com/march-fong-eu

CHAPTER THREE

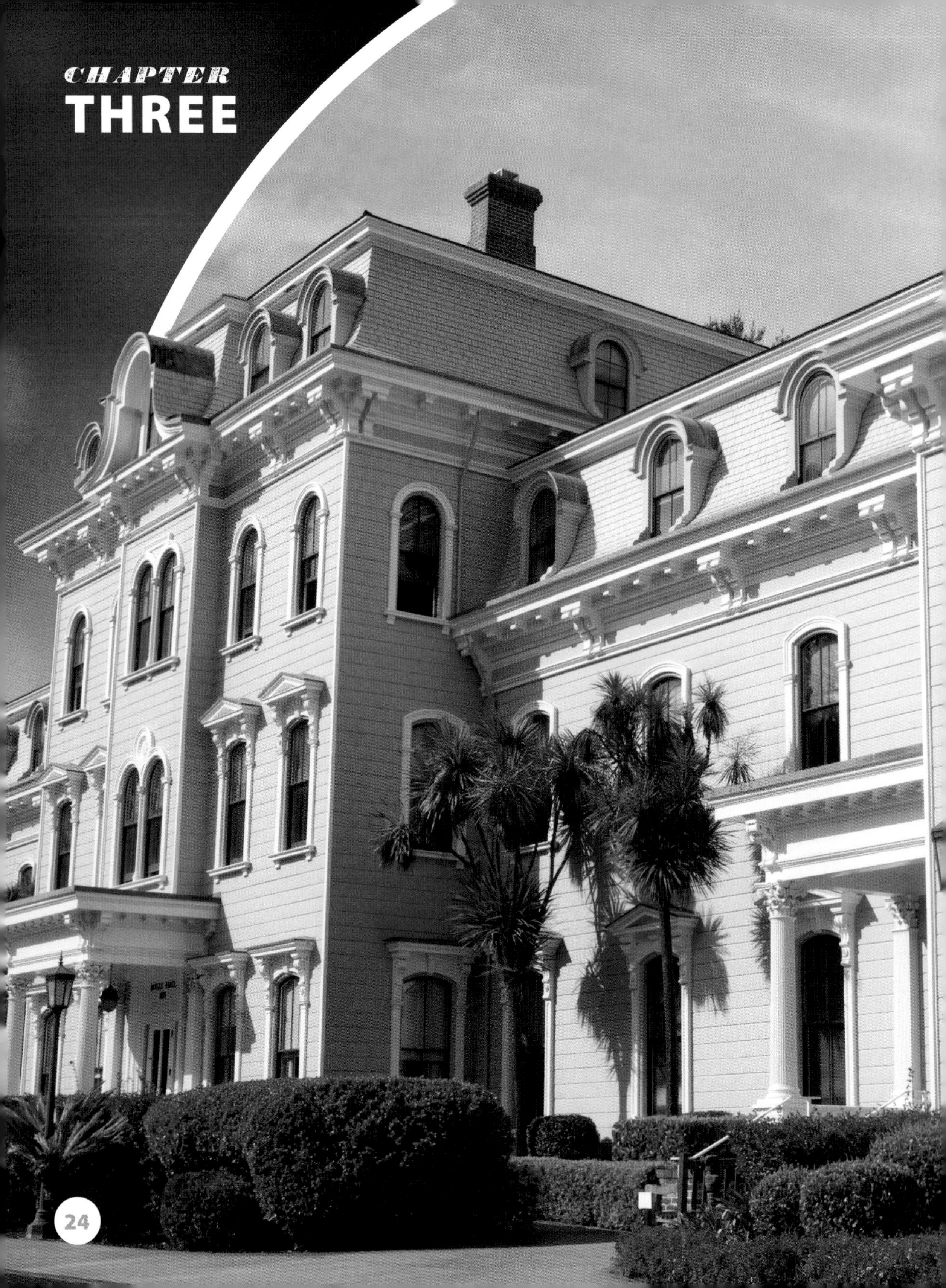

CHANGING CAREERS

March liked having new goals to pursue. In the 1940s, she decided to go to Mills College in Oakland to get a master's degree in health education. Getting an education helped her reach her goals. She believed teaching was a way she could help others achieve their goals too.

Meanwhile, March continued to work at the University of California, San Francisco. She also began teaching part-time in Alameda County, California. School officials put March in charge of dental health education. She prepared materials for teachers in the county

March attended Mills College in the 1940s. Mills College was founded as a school for women in 1852.

WOMEN IN COLLEGE

In the early and mid-1900s, women's job opportunities were limited. Women who wanted to work usually went into careers such as teaching or nursing. Because of this, more men than women attended college. Women's rights activists hoped to change this. They wanted women to have equal opportunities. After World War II, many colleges began expanding. They offered more career options, such as law and medicine. More women started going to college. In 1950, 32 percent of all college students were women. By the early 2000s, that number had risen to 57 percent.

to use. She also brought in dental hygiene students from the University of California to work in the schools.

In 1944 March became president of the American Dental Hygienists' Association. She served in the position until 1947. She earned her master's degree in the same year.

For March, this was the height of her dental career. She had advanced as far as she could in dentistry. At the time, women could not

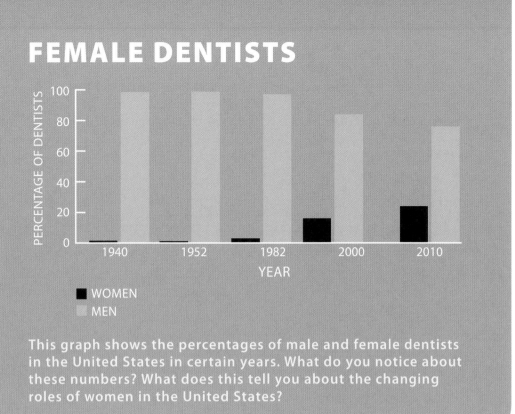

FEMALE DENTISTS

This graph shows the percentages of male and female dentists in the United States in certain years. What do you notice about these numbers? What does this tell you about the changing roles of women in the United States?

become dentists. Also, it was difficult for a woman to get into schools that taught a profession such as medicine or law. Many people expected that women who married would quit working to raise a family. They thought that women who went to professional schools would not use their education. For this reason, many professional schools did not accept women.

In 1948 the head of the University of California, San Francisco's department of dental hygiene passed away. The university offered March the position.

She accepted. She became the first woman and first Asian American to be head of the department. She served in the position until 1951.

FAMILY AND COMMUNITY

March decided to get a doctorate degree in education. She studied at Stanford University in California. She earned her degree in 1954.

In 1956 a new law was passed in Alameda County. It changed the process of how school board members were chosen. Before, the school superintendent had selected the school board members. The new law allowed county residents to choose a board member. When a seat opened up on the school board, people could campaign for the position. New school board members would be elected. March had worked in Alameda schools for a long time. She knew firsthand what the schools were like. She believed she could bring a new point of view to the school board.

March ran for an open position on the school board. The school superintendent supported her opponent, but March won anyway. Then March and her husband adopted a Chinese American baby boy named Matthew. They also adopted a Chinese American baby girl named Suyin. March decided it was a good time to retire. She wanted to stay home and care for her children. But she stayed involved in the community. She remained on the school board. She was also

PERSPECTIVES
THE SCHOOL BOARD

As an elected member of the school board, March had more freedom to speak out than those who had not been elected. The school superintendent had chosen most of the other board members. They often felt they had to agree with him on issues. But March felt free to disagree with him. She questioned many of the board's policies. She wanted to know about the board's budget and how money was spent. March did not see her position as a political job. She saw it as a way to keep serving the people in her community. She wanted to make decisions based on people's needs.

The League of Women Voters helped women register to vote in the 1920s. The group's mission today is to get people more involved in politics.

active in community organizations such as the League of Women Voters. As part of the League of Women Voters, she listened to people in her community. She gathered information about the political issues that were important to them.

While March served on the school board, she learned a lot about government and politics. She got to know many people in the state department of education. She learned how to talk to state legislators. She began to understand more about how laws are made. She also learned more about campaigning. March was president of the school board from 1961 to 1962. She served on the school board until 1964. Then she was ready for her next challenge.

STRAIGHT TO THE
SOURCE

March once spoke about how community involvement relates to politics. She said:

> I think you find, in many instances, [that] people who are in public office . . . have participated in a wide variety of community work. . . .
>
> So, politics really is an extension for a lot of people who start out just in their own communities. They find out in the process of their community activity that they can be more effective if they extend themselves beyond just the community. Then they somehow get into politics, and I guess they are encouraged by the people they work with, encouraged by them to go on to some other level of service where they can be of greater help.

Source: *March Fong Eu: High Achieving Nonconformist in Local and State Government.* Interviewed by Gabrielle Morris. Berkeley, CA: Regents of the University of California, 1978. 23. *Archive.org*. Web. Accessed September 16, 2019.

Consider Your Audience

Adapt this passage for a different audience, such as your friends. Write a blog post conveying this same information for the new audience. How does your post differ from the original text and why?

CHAPTER
FOUR

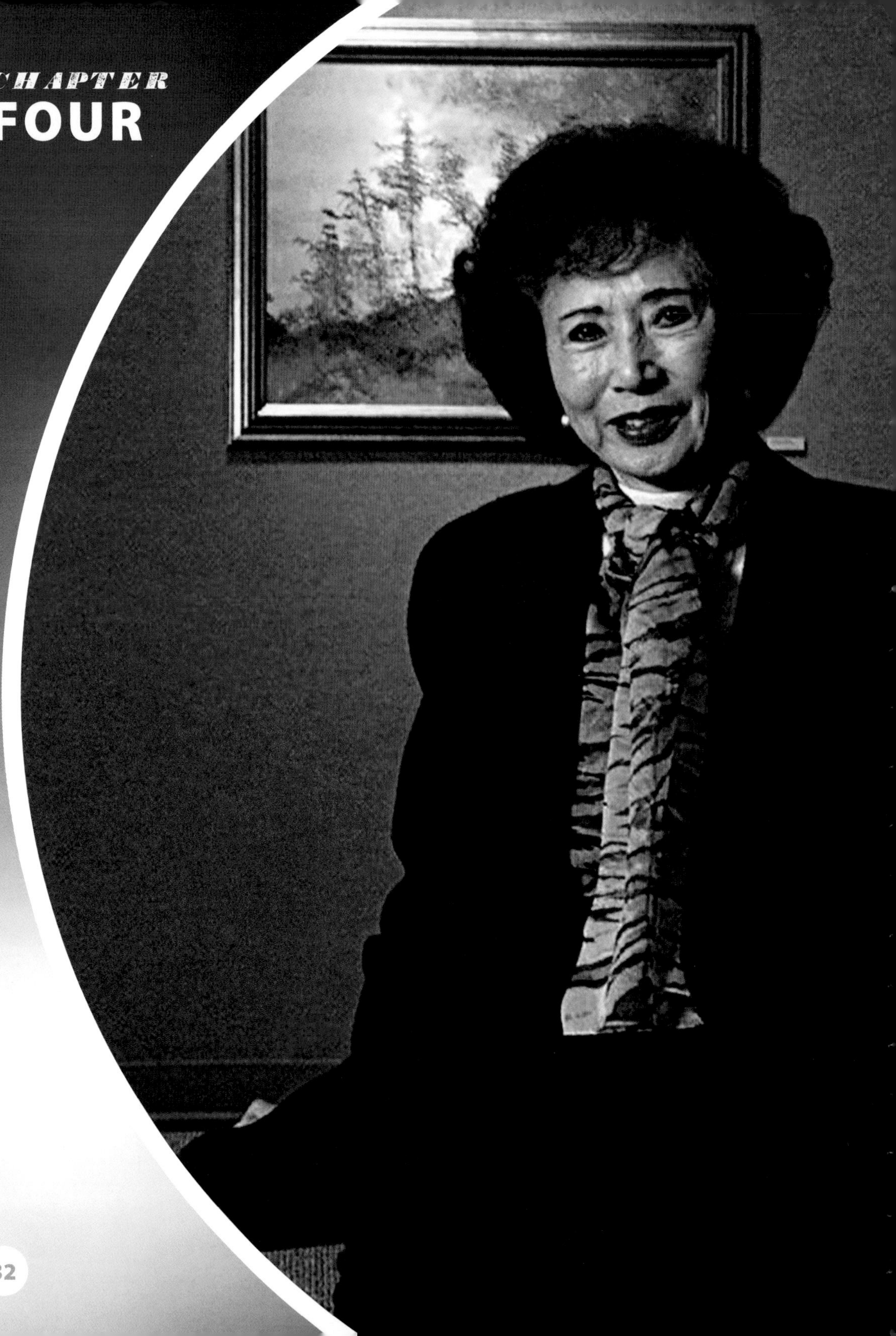

A PUBLIC SERVANT

I n 1966 March decided to run for the California State Assembly. First she had to win the primary election for her political party, the Democratic Party. If she won, she would run against the Republican candidate for the position. March spent a lot of time campaigning. She went from door to door and talked to people about the issues that mattered to them.

March wanted to win on her own merits. She refused to criticize her opponents. Instead she focused on her qualifications and ideas. March won the Democratic nomination.

March sits with her paintings displayed behind her. She enjoyed painting as a pastime.

Then she won the election. She received 58 percent of the votes.

FOCUSING ON THE ISSUES

In 1966 the positions in the assembly became full-time positions. The assembly met in the California State Capitol in Sacramento. March had to spend three nights each week away from home. Her husband worked at his dental practice. Her children were now in junior high school. A housekeeper took care of their home. March also had help from

March, *left*, supported other female politicians such as congresswoman Geraldine Ferraro, *third from right*.

her father-in-law. He lived with her family and ran the household while she was gone.

As a member of the assembly, March focused on many different issues. These included education, tax reform, and the state budget. March was also concerned about health policies, agriculture, and protecting the environment. Women's rights were important to her too. She encouraged women to get involved in politics. She believed male lawmakers would pay greater attention to women's issues if more women became politically involved.

One of March's most famous campaigns in the assembly was the fight against pay toilets. She was reelected to the assembly in 1968, 1970, and 1972. Each time, she won with more votes.

During this time, March and Chester divorced. In 1973 March married a businessman named Henry Eu. She took his last name and became March Fong Eu. The next year, she decided to run for the position of secretary of state. The secretary of state is the third-highest position in a state's government. A secretary of state serves under the governor and lieutenant governor. A woman had never served as California's secretary of state before. Many people did not think March could win. But her campaign was successful. She won the election.

A NEW WAY TO SERVE

As secretary of state, Eu oversaw voter registration and state elections. She started voter registration by mail.

Eu sits with Betty Ford, *right*, in 1976. Eu supported Betty's husband, President Gerald Ford, in his reelection campaign.

Eu, *right*, supported her son, Matt Fong, *middle*, when he ran for the California senate in 1998.

People who went through this process did not have to go anywhere to register. They could register to vote through the mail. This made the process easier. More people were able to become voters.

Eu also made changes to the rules for absentee ballots. People who are not able to vote in person at a polling place can vote ahead of time through an absentee ballot. There are many reasons someone may not be able to vote in person. Some voters may be out of town on Election Day. Others may be serving in the military. Eu allowed voters to use absentee ballots for any reason. These changes helped increase voter participation in elections.

Eu ran for secretary of state again in 1978 and won. She continued to be a popular secretary of state. She was reelected five times.

In 1988 Eu ran for a position in the US Senate. The candidates were required to share their family's financial history. But Eu's husband did not want to give out that information. Eu had to drop out of the race.

In 1994 President Bill Clinton gave Eu a new opportunity.

AN ACCOMPLISHED ARTIST

After taking a trip to Taiwan, Eu became interested in Chinese painting and calligraphy. When she retired from politics, she spent time improving her skills. She took lessons to learn Chinese brush painting. She wanted to connect to her Chinese roots. Eu also learned how to paint with oils. Oil paints are often used in European and American artwork. But Eu still focused on her heritage. She painted Chinese landscapes with cliffs and trees. She also painted fish and lotus ponds.

He appointed her the US ambassador to the Federated States of Micronesia. This nation is made up of 607 islands in the Pacific Ocean. Eu represented the United States in Micronesia. She helped support people in the country on behalf of the United States. Eu served in this position until 1996.

In 2002 Eu tried to win back her position as California's secretary of state. Although she lost that race, she had already accomplished so much. She helped break down barriers for women as they worked to gain equal rights. She also served as a role model for many Asian Americans.

Eu died on December 21, 2017. In honor of her contributions, California officials named the new secretary of state building after her in 2019. Today, people continue to recognize her legacy as a pioneering leader and activist.

STRAIGHT TO THE
SOURCE

In February 1973, Eu spoke to students at Foothill College in Los Altos Hills, California. Her speech was called "The Self-Sufficient Woman." She talked about women's involvement in politics:

In recent years we have witnessed a phenomenon unparalleled in our political history. Each year, more and more women are running—and more importantly—being elected to local, state and federal positions. . . .

The reasons for this trend are simple. Society is now able to recognize the fact that some women also possess the expertise needed to enter the political arena. With this, the notion of "a woman's place is in the home—or the oven" is ending.

Source: Dan Brekke. "March Fong Eu: 'The Self-Sufficient Woman.'" *KQED News*. KQED News, December 23, 2017. Web. Accessed May 29, 2019.

What's the Big Idea?
Take a close look at this passage. What is the connection Eu makes between women's empowerment and political involvement? How do these two ideas relate to each other?

FAST FACTS

- March Fong Eu was born in Oakdale, California, in 1922. She grew up in Richmond, California. Her parents owned a laundry business.

- Eu worked hard in school. She believed a good education would help her change her circumstances.

- She earned a bachelor's degree in dentistry, a master's degree in health education, and a doctorate degree in education.

- She worked hard for her community as a volunteer and a member of the school board.

- She ran for a spot on the California State Assembly in 1966. She won the election. She became the first Asian American woman to serve in a state legislature.

- In 1974 she ran for the position of California's secretary of state. She won the election. She was the first woman to be elected to this position. She served as secretary of state for nearly 20 years.

- Eu worked to help women gain equal rights. She also made the voting registration process easier.

- President Bill Clinton appointed Eu as the US ambassador to the Federated States of Micronesia in 1994.

- Eu died on December 21, 2017.

STOP AND
THINK

Tell the Tale

Chapter One of this book talks about the time March Fong Eu smashed a toilet on the steps of the California State Capitol. Imagine you were one of the people in the crowd when this happened. Write 200 words about the event and the crowd's reaction. What was the purpose of this action? Was it effective?

Surprise Me

Chapter Two discusses Eu's childhood and education. After reading the chapter, what two or three facts did you find most surprising? Write a few sentences about each fact. Why did you find each fact surprising?

Why Do I Care?

Maybe you are not old enough yet to vote in political elections. But that doesn't mean you can't think about political issues that are important to you. How did Eu's community involvement help her political career? How could you help your community?

GLOSSARY

absentee ballot
a ballot mailed to a person who cannot vote at a polling place

ambassador
a person sent to represent his or her country in another country

budget
an amount of money that is available to spend on something

calligraphy
an artistic style of handwriting

economy
a system in which goods and services are exchanged

gender discrimination
the act of treating people unfairly because of their gender

immigrant
someone who moves from one country to another to live there permanently

jury
a group of people at court trials that decides whether someone accused of a crime is guilty or innocent

labor union
a group of workers that advocates for better working conditions

ONLINE RESOURCES

To learn more about March Fong Eu, visit our free resource websites below.

Visit **abdocorelibrary.com** or scan this QR code for free Common Core resources for teachers and students, including vetted activities, multimedia, and booklinks, for deeper subject comprehension.

Visit **abdobooklinks.com** or scan this QR code for free additional online weblinks for further learning. These links are routinely monitored and updated to provide the most current information available.

LEARN MORE

Cunningham, Kevin. *How Political Campaigns and Elections Work.* Minneapolis, MN: Abdo Publishing, 2015.

Hopkinson, Deborah. *What Is the Women's Rights Movement?* New York: Penguin Workshop, 2018.

ABOUT THE AUTHORS

Duchess Harris, JD, PhD

Dr. Harris is a professor of American Studies at Macalester College and curator of the Duchess Harris Collection of ABDO books. She is also the coauthor of the titles in the collection, which features popular selections such as *Hidden Human Computers: The Black Women of NASA* and series including News Literacy and Being Female in America.

Before working with ABDO, Dr. Harris authored several other books on the topics of race, culture, and American history. She served as an associate editor for *Litigation News*, the American Bar Association Section of Litigation's quarterly flagship publication, and was the first editor in chief of *Law Raza*, an interactive online journal covering race and the law, published at William Mitchell College of Law. She has earned a PhD in American Studies from the University of Minnesota and a JD from William Mitchell College of Law.

Samantha S. Bell

Samantha S. Bell lives with her family in upstate South Carolina. She graduated from Furman University with a degree in history and a teaching certification in social studies. She is the author of more than 90 nonfiction books for children.

INDEX